**What people have**
**Digital Privacy Se**

CW00406268

"Extremely eye opening and interesting"

"A lot of very useful information - all of which I did not know
beforehand"

"Everyone should be aware of these critical issues"

"Highly informative and practical"

"Rather scary and thought provoking"

"John is clear, concise and to the point. His knowledge is well
deployed and he startles with the facts at the same time being
moderate and helpful."

"Vital and punchy"

"One of the most pressing issues we face explained in an
engaging and knowledgeable way."

"Authoritative, knowledgeable, and easy to understand - got the
message home, little jargon, great"

# Digital Privacy Self-defence

## Why it matters and what to do

John Nugent

The Institute for Digital Privacy

# About

The Institute for Digital Privacy ('IDP') is a digital privacy research and education enterprise for the protection of civil liberties and well-being. The IDP was founded by industry veteran John Nugent in 2018 and provides online and offline training seminars.

John has 25 years' experience in internet marketing and technology. He provides business and marketing strategy consulting in B2B marketing automation, B2C online marketing, and venture capital advisory. His former roles include founder of Voice Register (verified petition platform); Sector Head EMEA (Telco), Adobe; VP & GM EMEA Responsys (acquired by Oracle); Managing Director EMEA, DoubleClick (acquired by Google). He has lectured at the Institute for Data & Marketing and the University of the Arts. He was founder Chair of the IDM Social Media Council. He holds an LL.B (Hons) degree in law.

www.idigprivacy.com

*To Tracey,*
*Liam, Olivia & Patrick*
*with love*

# Table of Contents

# Introduction: Why worry?

*"If you have something that you don't want anyone to know, maybe you shouldn't be doing it in the first place."*

*- Eric Schmidt 2009, CEO & Executive Chair, Google 2001-2017; Chair, US Department of Defense Innovation Board 2016-2020; Chair, US National Security Commission on Artificial Intelligence 2019-*

Is privacy dead? As the mainstream media might have us believe. Are we wrong to trust websites? Perhaps their interests are not aligned with our own. Are we guilty when being private? Perhaps we should all be monitored, all of the time.

Actually research shows that we do care about privacy, with almost 80%[1] of us saying that we have strong concerns about our online privacy; and half[2] of us are faking personal data when using online services to protect our privacy and security. Contrary to popular belief, concern for our privacy is also not age related, with the young caring just as much as the old about their digital privacy[3].

The wealthier we are, the more privacy we usually seek to attain. Facebook-founder Mark Zuckerberg perfectly demonstrated this by spending $30 million to buy his four neighbouring houses for privacy[4]. Privacy is indeed a luxury and the word 'private' often prefixes high status, aspirational services such as private school, private hospital, or private plane.

However, the majority of people, who find ourselves in day-to-day crowded conditions, rely on purposefully pretending not to pay attention – or 'civil inattention' as defined by social scientist Irving Goffman. We ignore people to respect their privacy and we expect the same in return

And this subconscious, self-delusion of privacy stays with us when we go online – and is further enhanced by us normally being physically alone when we're on the internet.

In many liberal democracies privacy is also the law. In the UK our right to privacy is governed by Section 8 of the Human Rights Act 1998[5] – which originated from Article 12 of the United Nations Declaration of Human Rights 1948. As such, the 'nothing to hide' argument is based on the false premise that you don't have the right to privacy by default – that someone has already taken your privacy without consent.

However, the right to privacy is not an absolute right. Privacy is a 'qualified right' and as such, politicians are at liberty to reduce or modify our privacy rights for the purposes of national security, public safety, crime prevention or public health.

But changes to our right to privacy – or any other human rights - are almost always highly controversial. They are usually only attempted in times of actual or perceived national crisis, with the scale and duration of the change commensurate with the authoritarian tendencies of the government at the time. Given the politics of privacy, it's a welcome check on power that the law courts are the ones who have ultimate responsibility for deciding how our privacy interests are balanced.

# Digital Privacy Self-defence

The reason privacy is a right and a law in most democratic countries, is because privacy is a basic human need. It's instinctual.

Our sense of privacy starts at 18-24 months of age when we first develop a sense of self. A sense that we are separate from other people, that we have the autonomy to make personal decisions, and that not everything has to be shared. This process of forming our identity is often referred to by parents as 'the terrible twos'.

By the time we reach adulthood, our use of privacy to manage how we relate to others has become complex, pervasive and mostly unconscious. Privacy is the expected social norm in many situations and when it's violated we usually have, or receive, a strong negative reaction.

Privacy affords us the ability to demonstrate mutual respect. It enables us to create social boundaries based on different relationship types. It gives us the power to manage our reputation; and have second chances after minor indiscretions. It gives us freedom from having to constantly justify misinterpreted actions.

Privacy enables us to have trusted, confidential relationships. It gives us the power of self-control over our own data. It empowers our right to freedom of thought and speech that may differ from the current political or social norms. It empowers our right to associate with others to explore confidential or political ideas. And it provides a limit to political power – the authority for others to make decisions based on what they know about us.

When an authoritarian government grants itself unlimited political power and deprives a population of its privacy it operates as a 'surveillance state'... and living in a surveillance state is like living in a prison. Former citizens of East Germany that lived under the Stasi regime from the 1950s to the 1990s understand this better than most - and digital privacy remains a sensitive political issue in Germany today.

When the General Data Protection Regulations ('GDPR') were welcomed into force in 2018, the privacy of residents in the European Union became one of the most legally protected in the world. But it would be a mistake for us to rely on the law to protect our digital privacy. The internet is evolving significantly faster than politicians around the world can comprehend, co-ordinate and react with necessary legislation.

Tim Berners-Lee[6], the British computer scientist who invented the World Wide Web in 1990, has become a strong advocate for digital privacy. He believes that we should have the right to use the web in privacy just as we visit a doctor in privacy[7].

Unfortunately, Tim's 'claim to fame' was not originally designed with privacy in mind but he, and a whole host of other tech entrepreneurs, are now racing to bring privacy-friendly, alternative online services to market. Digital privacy self-defence solutions if you like.

# Part 1: The Digital Threat to Privacy

# How private is the internet?

The internet is a network of networks of computers – and every website we visit is on someone else's computer. Having to trust these websites with our data is the first privacy challenge.

Online services such as Facebook or Amazon are almost always centralised under the ownership of one private corporation - as opposed to decentralised where our data is not aggregated in one place, or even owned. The internet businesses of this world hum quietly in vast, deserted 'server farms', where we could perhaps be regarded as the livestock.

From a legal perspective, the internet is a network of contracts. There is no 'public' space on the internet. Every online service or app we engage with is private and necessitates a legal contract between us and the service provider. As you probably know from experience, we almost never read these terms and conditions and privacy policies before we agree to them.

For example, you may not realise that when you sign up for a Facebook account you give Facebook a perpetual, worldwide licence to use your content as they see fit. This is a common legal term on social media sites.

And this legal agreement goes to the heart of the difference between cyber security and digital privacy. Cyber security risks result from unauthorised activity like being hacked. But privacy risks usually arise after you authorise data processing by agreeing to a contract.

As older people may particularly appreciate, the software on our devices has replaced dozens of real-world tools like diaries, maps, clocks, newspapers, books, CDs & DVDs, train timetables, cameras and flashlights.

From the moment we wake up, travel, engage in work; and then socialise, exercise or entertain ourselves, software is managing and directing our day. There's an app for everything. And so every aspect of our day and our life is now managed and directed under service contracts with private organisations.

We share some of the most intimate data about ourselves with apps and online services, with the reasonable expectation that they would not be shared - from period trackers[8] through to our very genetic code[9]. But they *are* shared *and* sold. And the poorer we are, the less privacy we are given. Developing countries are specifically targeted with alternative apps that harvest their data in exchange for free services[10].

Often, we may not even have sight of the specific terms and conditions for software applications and online services that we use. Education institutions, for example, typically mandate the digital services pupils and students must use – which is usually Google, due to its ease of use and attractive zero financial cost. Any opt-out that you are offered is unlikely to lead to a viable, privacy-centric alternative. Under-resourced IT departments are rarely driven by privacy considerations and privacy is usually lacking from pupil safeguarding requirements[11].

And the same mandate is usually true for software we must use at work.

In 2012, Google took the decision to unite sixty of its privacy policies – including Search, YouTube and Gmail - into one, unifying privacy policy[12]. In 2016, a further privacy policy change allowed Google to combine its advertising network data with personally identifiable information. [13]

On the surface, these changes may have appeared to be a dull productivity exercise by the Google legal department... but the intention and effects were quite profound. Google was now able to claim that if you signed up to one of its services – like Gmail – it now had your consent to track and profile you wherever and whenever you knowingly or unknowingly used another Google service... and that, as will be revealed, happens to be most of the internet.

Multi-billion dollar consumer software technology companies like Google, Microsoft, Facebook, Amazon, Apple and others are know as 'Big Tech'. Understanding the Big Tech landscape is key to understanding our digital privacy challenges.

# The Big Tech landscape

The last twenty-five years have seen an explosion of digital innovation. Following the late-90s dotcom gold rush, the dotcom crash at the turn of the millennium was the start of what became a substantial market consolidation. From an early level playing field, companies such as Amazon, Google, Facebook, Netflix, AirBnB, Uber and TikTok have grown to dominate most of the traffic on the internet.

The capability of these Big Tech companies to innovate and rapidly expand globally has been remarkable, and on many levels admirable. The stuff of business school case studies and even sociological studies.

Taking lessons from the offline software industry before it, the tech giants played to win – in what turned out to be a winner takes all market. And in the view of Peter Thiel, founder of PayPal and Palantir, win meant build a monopoly[14].

The network effect played a large part in Big Tech rising to monopoly positions. The more people that used a platform the more useful the platform became, and the more brand recognition it achieved. The Big Tech businesses are now some of the most valuable brands in the world – with Apple at #1 position[15].

The power of network + brand can be demonstrated by Wikipedia – the not-for-profit anomaly. Wikipedia is one of the most visited websites on the internet but its terms and conditions allow you, surprisingly, to download a full copy of Wikipedia and put it on your own website if you wish[16]. It's testimony to the power of the online network + branding effect that such an act would be very unlikely to have any impact on Wikipedia's ongoing success.

It would undoubtedly be the same situation for the commercial Big Tech brands but their terms & conditions are unlikely to give you the opportunity to find out any time soon.

As innovative as the Big Tech companies have been, much of their success can be attributed to the venture capitalists that funded their growth. The US venture capital machine brought its full game to the internet business opportunity and has funded US tech companies to the tune of approximately $80B dollars per year[17].

Interestingly, Bono – the lead singer of the group U2 – was also the lead investor of a group that made more money out of buying early shares in Facebook than Bono made in 30-years from U2[18].

Less glamorous, but more strategically aligned with US economic interests, the CIA is also a major investor in internet businesses via its venture capital arm In-Q-Tel. Yes, the CIA has a venture capital arm. In-Q-Tel is particularly interested in supporting 'big data' businesses – businesses that aggregate and analyse data on citizens[19].

The reason venture capitalists have poured money into internet businesses is because internet businesses are fundamentally software companies. In 2011 Marc Andreessen, founder of Netscape, predicted that "in the future every company will become a software company" and "software is eating the world". The upshot of this is that businesses that fail to become software companies and transition to an internet-appropriate business model are unlikely to succeed.

Another way of looking at this, which seems to be playing out due to strategic and operational realities, is that a few Big Tech software companies will move into and take ownership of every other business. And it just so happens that American companies account for 91% of the total value of the world's top 300 software companies[20] - with Germany #2 at 1.8%. And that is a big, once in a century, money making opportunity for US venture capitalists.

The tech business strategy of 'get big, quick or go home' is certainly succeeding. Google has risen to monopoly-like positions in at least 12 separate business verticals including search, maps, mobile, video, translation, education, office suites, file storage, online advertising and email. Its market reach is such that there is Google code in an estimated 88% of all mobile apps[21] and 86% of all websites[22].

And Google – now under the umbrella of its parent company Alphabet – is showing no signs of a slowdown in ambition. Owning the artificial intelligence market is of particular interest and Google has spent $4 billion dollars acquiring 30 AI businesses prior to 2020. Given the data and funding at Google's disposal, it has a significant advantage in most digital markets it chooses to enter.

The power behind Google's advantage is the power of free. After early scepticism, Google founders Sergey Brin and Larry Page took the decision to fund Google by selling advertising to companies rather than imposing a charge on its users. This business model has given Google a winning competitive advantage when entering markets where users were being charged for services - such as office software, education software, maps or video distribution. In other words, Google changed consumer behaviour  from paying for products to expecting advertisers to fund their products for them.

Big Tech can broadly be divided into two business models. One is where you are the customer i.e. you pay for the product or service and are treated as the consumer. Apple, Amazon and Microsoft fall mostly into this category. In 2020, Apple made 80% of its revenue from hardware sales (mostly iPhones) and 15% of its revenue from digital content services like iTunes. Amazon made 80% of its revenue from retailing and 11% from web services. And Microsoft made 43% of its revenue from Windows and Microsoft Office and 24% from cloud hosting services.

The other Big Tech business model is where *you* are the product. In 2020, Google Alphabet made 86% of its revenue from selling advertising and Facebook made 99% of its revenue from selling advertising.

The most attractive clients to Google and Facebook are the big budget advertising agencies of the world's largest consumer brands such as Coca-Cola, Samsung, McDonald's or Toyota. Companies that spend billions on advertising each year.

But it's the long tail of lower budget clients, with more niche products and services, that make the most of Google and Facebook's operational goal – which is to acquire as much data about you as possible, so that advertisers can deliver increasingly more targeted messaging to you. This 'personalisation' is based on your perceived personal needs and wants. To quote Eric Schmidt, CEO of Google in 2010:

*"There is what I call the creepy line. The Google policy on a lot of things is to get right up to the creepy line and not cross it."*

To get hold of our data, two goals are given top business priority: (1) Make products as easy to use as possible and (2) make content as 'sticky' as possible – sticky being the Big Tech term for addictive. Google and Facebook are masters at both these disciplines; and TikTok a grand master. The more data they get, the more stuck we become[23].

Big Tech not only wants your data – it also wants you to reveal as much data about your family, friends and contacts as possible. These connections are known to Big Tech companies as your 'social graph'.

# Networked privacy

The nature of our social media platforms makes digital privacy not just a personal challenge but a collective or networked challenge.

One of the reasons Facebook knows so much about you – so much more than ever appears in your account – is that your family, friends and contacts have shared data about you… and in particularly, shared their address book. This 'people you may know service'[24] - to quote Kashmir Hill - has thrown up some bewildering anecdotes such as:

- *A man who years ago donated sperm to a couple, secretly, so they could have a child—only to have Facebook recommend the child as a person he should know. He still knows the couple but is not friends with them on Facebook.*
- *A woman whose father left her family when she was six years old who saw his then-mistress suggested to her as a Facebook friend 40 years later.*
- *An attorney who wrote: "I deleted Facebook after it recommended a man who was defense counsel on one of my cases. We had only communicated through my work email, which is not connected to my Facebook, which convinced me Facebook was scanning my work email.*

It's difficult to avoid apps and services that are bad for our privacy when they become popular with friends and family – or even become an everyday verb[25].

Our instinct as parents to share the achievements and cute moments of tour kids – 'sharenting' - is leaving an indelible footprint for many children. It's estimated that children have 1,300 pictures of themselves posted online by the age of 13[26]. And these images are not only used by the social media platforms but are now being acquired to create commercial databases for sale to marketers and law enforcement agencies for facial recognition purposes[27].

Governments also create large databases of our personal information to carry out civic tasks. For example, the UK's National Pupil Database is a detailed record of every child in every state school – including their sexual preference, religion and exam attainment data. This is retained indefinitely by the government and shared without our consent with universities, media companies and commercial organisations. The Department for Education received widespread criticism for sharing the personal details of 28 million children with betting companies for age verification purposes[28].

Even our National Health Service medical data is now being shared with Google[29] and Amazon[30].

Sometimes we hear that our data is being shared anonymously - without our personal details – as a re-assurance to our privacy concerns. But researchers have shown time and again that anonymized databases can very easy and accurately be de-anonymised[31].

# Online advertising vs privacy

The online advertising industry has proven to be a key adversary of digital privacy self-defence and understanding how it works will greatly enhance your ability to counter its threat.

Google and Facebook together own almost 60% of the digital advertising market[32]. It's a growing market and most advertising is now digital. Amazon is well positioned to significantly increase its advertising revenue share given its position as the #1 online retail website. And Microsoft has several media properties including LinkedIn and Bing that bring it advertising revenue. It also now serves adverts into its Windows operating system.

Telecoms companies like Verizon have also moved into the ad market - particularly in America where Internet Service Providers (ISPs) can sell customer data to advertisers[33].

Google not only makes advertising revenue from its own media properties but it also makes money from its online advertising network. Millions of websites monetise their content by serving adverts from the Google Display Network.

When Google acquired the advertising technology business DoubleClick in 2007 (disclosure: I was working for DoubleClick at the time) it gained an immediate 80% market share of the online display advertising market. If you install an ad blocker in your web browser you'll often see Google's DoubleClick branded cookies being blocked, along with the names of many other independent ad network cookies.

Beyond regular advertising, online marketing networks also come in the form of affiliate networks and content syndication networks. Affiliate networks enable member websites to earn commission from referral sales when you click on a link. Amazon's affiliate network is the largest example.

Content syndication networks are used for content marketing i.e. where content rather than adverts are placed on websites.

These advertising networks, with their built-in trackers, often reach behind secure logins. For example, as of 2020, if you log-in to Experian to check your personal credit score you are subject to trackers from Google's DoubleClick, Facebook, Twitter and many others. Ironically Experian advise you to 'close your browser when you leave Experian... due to the sensitive nature of the information and data within this site'.

Together these advertising platforms and marketing networks collect, aggregate and licence our data. Wherever possible they do so by linking it to our personal identity such as an email address or phone number that we have shared, or by the identity of a device we are using.

Our online data is increasingly merged with our offline data and brokered by traditional database marketing companies such as Acxiom – who even sell its data to Facebook[34].

How does online advertising work? Well, in the split second it takes for a new web page to appear in your web browser when you click on a link, an auction has taken place. The website's ad serving technology has auctioned your page view to hundreds of advertisers. The advertiser that was willing to pay the most for a potential click by you on their advert wins the auction and their advert is displayed on the web page.

If you do click on their ad – which only about 1 in 1,000 people will do - they'll usually pay somewhere between 50 pence and five pounds for your 'click-through'. The price depends on your profile data and the value of the product they're selling. For example, financial services adverts to people known or inferred to be wealthy are probably the highest click value. Consumer commodities that aren't individually bought online, such as a soap brand, would have the lowest click-through value.

Before the internet came along, marketers bought adverts in the media based on the relevance of their product to the likely readership or viewership of that media. And readership was identified by using market research. For example, a luxury skiing holiday advert might perform well in the Sunday Telegraph Travel supplement; and a loan advert might perform best in a budget tabloid like the Daily Star.

But if you wanted to advertise to a more specific target market you would favour sending direct mail to consumer households. This is also known as database marketing because it relied on marketers selecting their mailing list based on data - such as average income by postcode, age, gender, your credit score or past products that you'd bought. Most of us call this 'junk mail'. The modern version of this is email marketing – sent legitimately when you've subscribed or illegitimately through spam when you haven't.

Advertising on the internet is now almost entirely driven by this database marketing approach – using information about individuals or groups to target ads rather than website readership type data. And the information about us is now so detailed that people can be targeted not only on demographics, like age or gender, but on psychographics like your interests or attitudes. You can even be targeted based on your perceived mental health[35].

This switch from media-based advertising to audience-based advertising is proving fatal for most traditional media companies that lack the big data acquisition capability of Google and Facebook.

Your email address is a valuable tool for marketers to uniquely identify you and match different data sets about you – as indeed is your mobile phone number. For example, marketers that have acquired your email address (perhaps through a transaction, an email newsletter subscription or a membership) can upload your email address to Facebook so that their adverts are only shown to that list and no one else. You can see the companies that have done this in your Facebook account settings.

Advertising has now been taken to its logical extreme of targeted advertising to just one person. There are online advertising companies that now enable you to advertise to your husband or wife, boyfriend, girlfriend, or even your boss… to influence their propensity to agree with you or to take an action you desire[36].

The goal of advertising is to get us to buy stuff – products or opinions. And the internet has taken personalisation to such a level of sophistication that its reasonable to agree with computer scientist Jaron Lanier's conclusion that the online media industry is best described as 'a behaviour modification empire':

*"We cannot have a society in which, if two people wish to communicate, the only way that can happen is if it's financed by a third person who wishes to manipulate them,"* he says[37].

Behaviour modification is what some governments now call 'nudging'.

One of UK Prime Minister David Cameron's less visible achievements was to set up the Behavioural Insights Team (BIT) at the Cabinet Office in 2010[38] – more commonly known as the 'Nudge Unit'. The Nudge Unit was nick-named after Thaler & Sunstein's bestselling book 'Nudge' which was about the power of subconsciously influencing people's decisions. The goal of the Nudge unit is to increase citizen compliance with government policies by combining the psychology of nudging with the execution capabilities of personalised digital media.

# Web Services vs privacy

Alongside online advertising, the web services industry is also a key adversary in digital privacy self-defence and understanding how it works is worth some exploration.

Developers and programmers who build websites and apps almost never do so by writing all the code from scratch. Most will use 3rd party web services and pre-written code to create their final solutions. The world of APIs and SDKs. Many of these services are provided – usually for free – by Big Tech companies like Google and Amazon.

One of the privacy challenges we face is that often developers don't know how the services and code used in their apps deal with data privacy – either because of time and budget constraints or because access to such insights is not available to them[39].

Two of the most popular web services used by websites are Google Analytics and Google reCAPTCHA. Google Analytics provides technical and marketing insights with regards to how a website is used and where website visitors are coming from. It works seamlessly with the Google AdWords' advertising platform which almost every marketer needs in their online advertising campaigns.

Google reCAPTCHA is designed to identify you as a real person – as opposed to an automated webcrawler - when filling in a form on a website for example. It's a particularly popular ID check with website owners but particularly annoying for users averse to helping Google Street View identify traffic lights, road signs or shops.[40]

Google Analytics and Google reCAPTCHA are two of the biggest threats to online privacy as they give Google the capability to track you across most of the internet with a significant level of detail.

Social login is another web service that creates privacy problems. When you're nudged into the convenience of using your Facebook log-in to create an account with a website, you may not realise it but you are granting permission to that website to access your personal details on Facebook – including your friends and family social graph information[41]. You can view and manage these websites in your Facebook account. Google has a similar capability.

It's not just commercial organisations that use web services. Developers creating government websites often bake in 3rd party services from Big Tech companies. For example, in 2020 London's Westminster Council's website was using the popular Google Fonts service, which shares your IP address with Google, and both Google and Facebook social log-in options which share much more.

At a larger scale than web services is software-as-a-service ('SaaS') solutions. These are online applications such as website content management systems, website personalisation engines and email marketing solutions that businesses use to run their websites and apps. Just three companies dominate the provision of SaaS to most large businesses: Adobe (of Photoshop fame), Salesforce and Oracle.

These B2B (business-to-business) services can sometimes be seen in your cookie or blocked cookie list, but are often hidden, behind-the-scenes players. They each have thousands of clients paying in the region of £30,000 to £300,000 per year for each SaaS service they use.

To go deeper, behind the websites are the cloud platforms where the websites are hosted. These data centres, or server farms, take away the headache and capital costs of companies managing their own servers. Again, just three vendors dominate this market for infrastructure as a service: Amazon, Microsoft and Google[42]. On average, one-in-three websites you visit will be hosted on Amazon servers; and Amazon generated ~$26 billion a year in revenue from Amazon Web Services in 2020.

At its deepest level, below the cloud hosting layer is a global network of undersea cables that form the base of the internet's data transmission infrastructure. There are over a million miles of fibre optic cables that transmit our data at the speed of light – making websites instantly accessible wherever they are in the world.

This network has historically been owned by telecoms companies like AT&T and Liberty Global (the US cable company behind the UK's Virgin Media brand). However, Big Tech is now moving into owning its own Tier 1 cable. Facebook, Microsoft, Amazon and Google – often in partnership – continue to lay undersea cables across the North Atlantic, South Atlantic, North Pacific, South Pacific and India Ocean[43].

Owning the main cables, and space satellites[44], over which all our data is transmitted could give Big Tech an unrestricted view of our digital lives... along with government security services[45], of course.

# Why are we being profiled?

The answer to this question is that corporates are vying to own our digital self. To quote activist Aral Balkan 'data about people is people' ... and owning 'digital people' gives Big Tech the power to control real people.

Most Big Tech products and services are designed with this end in mind; and Big Tech companies are in a race to create the most detailed and live digital version of each and every one of us.

Working in the tech industry is not without excitement and challenge. Tech employees are at the heart of the information revolution which will shape the next stage of our human development. But at the end of the day, the reason Big Tech wants to own digital people is because owning digital people makes for trillion dollar company valuations – the next goal after hitting billion dollar 'unicorn' status.

And that puts Big Tech founders into the Richest People on Earth club.

The reason governments are attracted to owning digital people is the power and security that having ultimate control over citizens brings. And Big Tech businesses lobby politicians to pursue these interests - and win lucrative service contracts as a result. For example, in 2015, Amazon won a $600m contract to provide cloud computing services to the CIA[46].

Security in this way doesn't even require constant surveillance. As Jeremy Bentham's Panopticon demonstrated with prison design, the mere thought that someone may be watching you will chill your behaviour. And chilled behaviour promotes compliance.

The internet enables the ultimate feedback loop for chilling people's behaviour, bringing them in line with business interests, social norms or authoritarian ideals. The State of California publishing the 'Delinquent Taxpayers List' or China showing public videos of citizens caught jay walking are two fine examples of this public shaming technique. A technique that has also fuelled the tabloid newspaper industry for decades.

# How is your data used?

Big Tech decides what we see and when we see it. Proprietary algorithms (sets of rules in software) determine the products and content we're shown. This is based on what the website knows about our digital selves and our social graph – along with business priority nudging.

These algorithms are usually designed and trained to show us more of what or who we like - to 'personalise' our experience. But we may also find ourselves in a 'filter bubble' (as coined by author Eli Parser) that prevents our exposure to new products, services, people or ideas.

Facebook runs a proprietary algorithm in its news feed called EdgeRank and decides which of your friends see which of your posts. This is based on what those friends consciously or unconsciously like or dislike about what you're posting. The result is that an estimated 65% of your friends don't see your posts[47]. In this way, Facebook can mediate our friendships – for better or worse.

Certainly, there are benefits to these algorithms which is what makes them so widely accepted. Personalisation can be very useful to help you decide what products to buy from a choice of hundreds. It might be comforting to only have people recommended to you that look like people you already follow - as the TikTok algorithm has been shown to do[48]. Collective data can also be used for social benefit such as helping to find the cure for major diseases[49].

But maybe your personal data is being used to make things more expensive – such as Uber knowing you'll pay surge pricing if your phone battery is at 5%[50]. Or your data could impact your ability to get a loan because your social graph has too many friends with a low credit score – an ability which Facebook has patented[51].

Or your personal data could impact your career, with 45% of recruiters saying that negative or inappropriate social media comments will go against you when applying for a job. But before you shut down your account, 17% of recruiters say that having no social media presence will also go against you[52].

Your data could also be used to make you sad. Famously, Facebook ran an experiment on 700,000 users to measure the impact of being shown either only negative or only positive posts in their newsfeed (accomplished by a tweak to the EdgeRank algorithm). Users did in fact become either more negative or more positive in their behaviour based on the content they were exposed to[53].

Your data can be be used to change how you vote. In 2010 Facebook ran a randomised control trial on 61 million people encouraging them to vote on the day of the US congressional election[54]. This single initiative generated an estimated 341,000 additional votes. To put this in context, the 2000 US presidential election between George Bush and Al Gore came down to just 537 votes in Bush's favour.

Research in 2020 by Dr Robert Epstein has revealed that Google's "autocomplete" feature on its search engine can turn a 50/50 split among undecided voters into nearly a 90/10 split — all without people realizing they're being manipulated[55].

Your data could make you a criminal suspect. Google reported a cyclist to the police that Google had tracked regularly cycling past a house that was subsequently burgled[56]. The cyclist proved to be innocent.

Your data could subject you to state punishment in some countries. The Chinese people live under a regime of constant social credit scoring. The more compliant you are as a citizen, the higher your score. If your score becomes too low you can be punished – perhaps receiving an automated ban from the use of public transport[57].

Your data could prove to be lethal. In April 2014, US General Michael Hayden, a former director of both the CIA and the NSA, said: "We kill people based on metadata"[58] using drone strikes. He then qualified that stark assertion by reassuring the audience that the US government doesn't kill American citizens on the basis of their metadata.

All of these uses of data rely to a greater or lesser extent on algorithms. But a key problem with algorithms making decisions is that they are not impartial arbiters. Beyond purposeful nudging, the biases and errors of the people that create algorithms have resulted in racist and sexist outputs[59].

# Privacy blows up

In 2013 privacy blew up. Edward Snowden, a technology contractor working for the firm Booz Allen at the US National Security Agency (NSA) became a whistle blower... or traitor depending on your point of view.

Snowden revealed that a network of countries had created a global mass surveillance system for the internet – led by the US, UK, Australia, New Zealand and Canada (named the 'Five Eyes')[60]. It was revealed that Big Tech data had become government data. The US Big Tech companies had been sharing their data with US security agencies, either knowingly or unknowingly[61]. This initiative had originated days after the 9/11 terrorist attacks, when the US Patriot Act gave the security services the unprecedented power to do so.

In the UK, it was revealed that the government security service GCHQ had been illegally monitoring all UK internet traffic[62]. The UK government rushed legislation through parliament to make its actions legal which - following various abuses, legal challenges and iterations - resulted in the Investigatory Powers Act 2016 (IPA)... otherwise known as the 'Snoopers Charter'.

The IPA requires your ISP and mobile network to retain all of the last 12-months of your internet data. It gives over 60 government and non-government bodies the ability to access your data, with some basic oversight. As you might expect these include law enforcement and security services, but as you may not expect they also include HMRC, the Department of Work and Pensions, the Food Standards Agency and the Gambling Commission.

And thus we have entered a new era, defined by Harvard Business School Professor Dr Shoshana Zuboff, as the 'Age of Surveillance Capitalism'… where "once we searched Google, now Google searches us".

Self-censoring behaviour began following Snowden's revelations, Wikipedia measured a 20 percent decline in page views related to the word 'terrorism'[63]. The 'chilling effect'.

At the same time, web browser ad blocking technologies took off. People realised that the online advertising industry and Big Tech was part of a global surveillance network.

Philosophical questions were subsequently asked: "Are we going to allow a means of communications which it simply isn't possible to read? My answer to that question is: 'No we must not.'" stated UK Prime Minister David Cameron in response to a terrorist attack in Paris in 2014[64]. In other words, digital private conversations should not be allowed.

So privacy was redefined, to quote Federike Kaltheuner of Privacy International:

*'Privacy was once misconstrued as being about hiding and secrecy. Now it is understood to be about something much more pressing: about power dynamics between the individual, the state and the market.'*

In 2019 a report by the world's leading human rights organisation, Amnesty International, came straight out with it:

*"Facebook and Google's omnipresent surveillance of billions of people poses a systemic threat to human rights."*[65]

# Part 1 Summary

In Part 1 we looked at how the internet is a private space with our everyday lives now under contract. And how a few Big Tech giants dominate the internet with their consumer services, advertising networks and web services – which collectively track and profile us... creating digital versions of ourselves.

We learned how our digital selves are used to beneficially personalise our services but are at the mercy of far less benign intentions which quietly nudge or socially shame us.

And we learned how Edward Snowden changed everything with his revelation of government mass surveillance hand-in-hand with Big Tech.

Our freedoms now depend on us taking digital privacy self-defence action.

# Digital Privacy Self-defence

# Part 2: How Do We Protect Our Digital Privacy?

# Digital Privacy Self-defence

As we've seen, corporations, namely Big Tech corporations, are at the top of our list of privacy adversaries. Hackers are largely amateurish in comparison but the damage they can cause does require us to take steps to improve our cyber security in order to protect our privacy.

Protecting your privacy from corporations will go a long way to protecting your privacy from governments. That said, to the extent that a government is lawfully carrying out its civic duty to provide services they will require your data.

When thinking about online privacy it's important to distinguish the level of anonymity you need based on your threat level. Most people do not require complete anonymity online – which would require you to disassociate your device purchases, your online activity and your location from your real identity.

This 'state surveillance' level of protection requires extreme measures which are unlikely to be justified unless you are a freedom fighter or a criminal. The primary threat most people are looking to mitigate is everyday, unwanted tracking and profiling – and most, but by no means all, of the tactics we'll now discuss would be a low barrier to targeted surveillance by state security services.

Privacy is a self-improvement task – like learning a new sport, an instrument or becoming a vegetarian. Think about digital privacy as an initial 20-hour project spread over a few weeks. This will give you enough time to get your head around what needs to be done and learn how to do it.

You don't need to be particularly technical to significantly improve your privacy but some of the more advanced tactics require a reasonable level of confidence – and you may benefit from asking a tech-savvy friend or family member to help you if you get stuck.

The tactics we are about to discuss are a solid foundation in understanding the threats to your privacy and the types of solutions you can use in its defence. However, both threats and software are constantly changing and specific solutions and settings do become outdated. Once you know what to look for, you should take a moment to research and verify the latest information online before making any significant changes to your devices, services or software.

As you gain understanding, let your contacts know about the basic steps they can take to avoid sharing your data without your consent; and in return, sharing your digital privacy self-defence knowledge will help your family and friends also stay safe.

# Digital privacy fundamentals

When thinking about digital privacy self-defence, there are several fundamentals to look for that will help you assess the privacy level of a product or service.

1) Was the service created as a privacy alternative?

If the service markets itself as a privacy alternative to an existing Big Tech service, that is always a good start. For example, DuckDuckGo.com markets itself as a privacy alternative to using the Google search engine. Given its relative lack of surveillance capability or aspirations, DuckDuckGo largely fulfils on its privacy promise but, as a US-based company subject to government data laws, it doesn't get an A grade.

2) Is the business model NOT audience advertising

If the online service makes money by acquiring your data for personalised advertising it cannot, by definition, respect your privacy. StartPage.com launched in 1998 with a 'no tracking' promise and became a popular search engine for privacy advocates. It uses Google search results but acts as an anonymising proxy between the user and Google. It does make money by selling advertising but does so purely related to search terms rather than personal data.

3) Is the service decentralised?

Most online services we use are centralised i.e. they're under the ownership of one private corporation which holds our data like Facebook or Amazon for example. Decentralised services are where there are multiple instances of the software that are not under single ownership and that inter-operate. The software could be federated across multiple servers or the software could be running on your actual device as a distributed app ('Dapp').

Decentralised services have privacy baked-in because there is no central oversight of your data and your data may never even leave your own laptop. For example, an alternative to Amazon.com or eBay that runs a decentralised service is OpenBazaar. It runs on your laptop and allows you to buy and sell goods with no central intermediary – otherwise known as a peer-to-peer ('P2P') model. This was the original way Skype worked before Microsoft acquired Skype and routed all communications through its central servers, thereby removing its inherent privacy.

It's still early days for decentralised services but do try them where you can.

4) Is the tech Free and Open Source Software ('FOSS')?

Most of the software that you use is likely to be proprietary i.e. it's owned by a company, costs money, cannot be legally copied, and gives no access to its source code (how it's written). For example, Microsoft Windows, Microsoft Office, Apple IoS, Photoshop and most apps on your phone are proprietary.

Free and open source software ('FOSS') is software that is not owned by a company. It's free - as in money but also free as in liberty - because it gives you a legal licence to use and amend the software as you wish. Effectively you own it when you download it.

Being able to access the source code of FOSS means that developers and security professionals can check if the software is spying on the user or not i.e. whether it is 'malware' that is designed to cause harm. This is the opposite of the proprietary model of 'security by obscurity' which requires you to simply trust that the proprietary software is not spying on you because you cannot verify otherwise.

FOSS is developed by communities of developers for their own benefit and for the benefit of others – in the same way that Wikipedia is created by the community and everyone benefits.

The Linux and original Android operating systems are examples of free and open source software. Much of the internet runs on free and open source software such as the Linux operating system, Apache Web Server or WordPress content management software. Linux is extremely stable and efficient – which is why 100% of the world's top 500 super computers run on Linux. There is almost always a FOSS version of popular proprietary software that you might be using.

5) Does the service use end-to end encryption?

Encryption is the method by which information is converted into secret code that hides its true content. Without encryption our communications over the internet can easily be intercepted and read by corporations, governments and hackers.

Here's how encryption works: When Alice and Bob use software that encrypts their messages to each other, the software creates a public key and a private key pair for each of them. Each person's key pair is unique to them. When Alice sends Bob a message, Alice's software uses Bob's public key to encrypt her message on her laptop before sending it over the internet to Bob. Anyone intercepting this message will be unable to de-crypt the message because modern encryption is usually too strong for current computing capabilities. When Bob receives Alice's message his private key can unencrypt the message because his private key works with – and is the only key in existence that works with - his public key.

Encryption is used whenever a secure connection is required online – such as when you enter credit card details on a website, use a banking app or use a secure messaging app for example. Most websites turn on encryption by default with a HTTPS connection displayed on their web address in your web browser. Without encryption your security and privacy are compromised.

6) Is there a government encryption back door?

Unfortunately, governments around the world have recently been calling for – and in Australia's case legislating[66] for - encryption 'back doors'. These back doors give the government an extra key that enables them to intercept and read any encrypted communication. Governments claim they need back-doors to prevent crime and terrorism but most cyber security and privacy experts are strongly opposed to such initiatives as they provide successful hackers with a master key – and allow governments to carry out mass surveillance.

7) Does the service's jurisdiction afford legal protection?

The GDPR 2018 legislation provides data protection to all EU citizens regardless of the jurisdiction the website falls under – in effect, forcing most popular websites to comply with GDPR.

This is a welcome position for EU residents but a controversial position with most non-EU websites.

As such, ensuring compliance and enforcement for any wrong doings on web businesses outside the EU is, at best, challenging. Try to ensure that the jurisdiction stated in the terms and conditions of a website is based in a country with strong privacy legislation, a legal system that is robust, and has a respectful demeanour towards the EU.

8) Are different brands linked?

A key cyber security principle which applies to privacy is 'security by isolation & compartmentalisation'. Online this means minimising your use of multiple services that originate from one provider – as your data is likely to be linked and shared if you do so.

For example, using Google's Chrome web browser on a Google Android phone to search Google.com for a Google YouTube video that you share with a friend via Google's Gmail is about as bad as it gets for your data privacy.

# Where are you at risk?

There are six key areas where your digital privacy is at risk:

1. Your personal devices
2. 'Smart devices' that you buy
3. 'Smart cities' that you live in
4. Your network connections to the internet
5. Your web browsing activity
6. The software applications that you use

Before expanding on these areas, it's worth noting that keeping your operating systems and applications up to date is a fundamental requirement for cyber security. The dark side of the hacking community is very quick to exploit known security vulnerabilities in old software. To avoid forgetting to update, set your operating system and applications to automatically download security updates and prompt you to install them.

Also worth noting is that most MS Windows users think that anti-virus software will protect them from cyber-crime, whereas almost no security experts would agree – with many experts regarding anti-virus software as privacy malware.[67]

# Personal devices: Computers

The computer operating system market is dominated by Microsoft Windows with 72% market share. Apple comes in at 16%; and Linux at 3%[68].

Which operating system is most private? Linux.

With the introduction of Windows 10, Microsoft took the strategic decision to basically make Windows a hybrid desktop and cloud system - with data flowing between your laptop and Microsoft's servers at many levels. Microsoft has also chosen to allocate an advertising ID to each Windows 10 installation – serving adverts into your applications. By default, Windows also uploads everything you type to Microsoft. And even if you take the considerable time and effort to implement every Windows privacy setting you can, updates are liable to change your settings. Most viruses and malware in the world also target Windows users. In short, Windows is a privacy nightmare.

Apple's macOS is a considerable improvement on Windows 10, not least because it's relatively untouched by viruses and malware. Apple also gets privacy points for not focusing on the advertising business. However, Apple loses points by having an increased focus on cloud uploads and by linking together data from its devices. Apple is also not free and open source software so, like Windows, we must trust they have best intentions towards our privacy.

Linux has all the benefits of FOSS and is not linked to advertising or the cloud. For newcomers, an easy to use Linux operating system is the free Ubuntu desktop.

If you're new to Linux operating systems, an easy way to get comfortable with Ubuntu is to watch an 'Introduction to Ubuntu' video on YouTube. You can then download and start Ubuntu from a USB stick in your laptop and have a look around. When you're ready to commit, click on Install and select the option to run alongside Windows. This keeps Windows (and all your files and settings) on your machine but also adds Ubuntu – creating what's called a 'dual boot' machine. Every time you then start or restart your computer you'll have an option screen to either select to run Ubuntu or select to run Windows.

This is a great way to switch to Ubuntu while keeping the utility of the Windows operating system you're familiar with. And over time you'll learn to use Windows less and less. Ubuntu uses significantly less computer resources than Windows and is great to install on older laptops to make them run like new.

Another way of installing Ubuntu is to first install a virtual machine ('VM') software programme such as VirtualBox on your current operating system. VirtualBox then enables you to install and run any operating system within it. Virtual machines make switching between operating systems quicker than dual booting; and are the easier way for Apple Mac users to install Ubuntu, rather than dual booting. Your privacy is best served by running a Windows 'Guest OS' inside your Ubuntu 'Host OS', rather than vice-versa, once you are ready to switch to Linux as your primary operating system.

Linux operating systems come in many flavours or 'distributions' as they are called. Whonix is a version of Linux that is very privacy focussed because it runs all internet access over the encrypted Tor network, which we'll cover later. It also separates your network connection from the operating system, so that if your web browser is ever compromised, your real IP address is not discoverable. Whonix is probably not for day-to-day use for most people but once you're comfortable with Ubuntu and VirtualBox, Whonix as a virtual machine will give you optimal privacy.

Another Linux distribution you should be aware of for privacy and anonymity is Tails. Tails runs on a USB stick, so saves nothing to the laptop hard drive. When you disconnect the USB stick or shut down your laptop all history, downloads and settings are also erased from the USB. Tails is an acronym for The Amnesic Incognito Live System because it forgets everything and leaves no trace. Ideal for freedom fighters in oppressive regimes who may be subject to government forensic analysis of their laptop hard drives.

As we've seen, with a virtual machine you can run a guest operating system on top of your host operating system. The Qubes operating system takes this concept to the next level by running each of your applications inside its own, separate operating system. If you're an above average Linux user with plenty of RAM on your machine, Qubes is the ultimate way to isolate and compartmentalise for security and privacy.

Choosing the right laptop has privacy implications.

The leading laptop for hardware and software privacy is probably the Librem range from Purism. Librem laptops are designed for privacy – with open source hardware components, hard switches for turning off the webcam and microphone, open source firmware, and the open source Linux distribution operating system PureOS.

As we've seen, you can install a Linux operating system like Ubuntu on your PC laptop to significantly improve your privacy and security. Or you can use an Apple MacBook, perhaps also running Whonix in a virtual machine, for when maximum privacy is needed.

Both the FBI and Mark Zuckerberg are advocates of covering up your laptop webcam with a privacy slider - especially for Windows users, who are statistically most likely to get hacked.

And you should turn on hard drive encryption, ideally when first installing an operating system. This prevents your data being accessible if you lose your laptop – as long as it was completely turned off when you lost it.

I'd recommend re-installing your operating system perhaps once a year to minimise security and privacy risks that may have got through your defences. This is easy to do with a free Linux operating system.

# Personal devices: Mobiles

Your smartphone is a marvel of sensing and tracking. It contains more senses than the human body – including a magnetometer that measures the Earth's magnetic field and a barometer that measures air pressure. It contains many ways to track your location including satellite GPS, cell phone tower triangulation and, indirectly, Bluetooth and Wi-Fi.

Most of the data that your phone is constantly generating – along with the data that you choose to put on your phone is accessible, to varying degrees, by the phone manufacturer, the operating system, and the network provider.

Many of the apps on your phone have been pre-installed and cannot easily be removed. These too can access the phone's data, along with any additional apps you choose to download. And your web browsing privacy is no less challenged than when browsing on your laptop.

Of course you do have to agree to all those terms and conditions and privacy policies but, if you're like most people, you agreed but you did not read. And even if you did read, you almost certainly had no choice other than to accept the legal terms to have a working phone or install a popular app.

Mobile phone privacy is a 'best efforts' endeavour, at best.

Your phone network constantly triangulates and records your location when your mobile phone connects to phone tower signals. This data can be shared with police and security services. But it can also be accessed by hackers exploiting major vulnerabilities in the worldwide 'SS7' mobile phone infrastructure. With just your phone number hackers can listen to calls, read SMS and track your detailed movements[69].

In 2019, The New York Times engaged a hacker to do just this and published images of individual cell phone movements inside high security buildings, including the Pentagon in Washington D.C.[70]

It's also relatively trivial and inexpensive to set up a fake cellphone tower to do the same thing. Police use fake towers for monitoring criminals, demonstrations and the like. Hackers can use them too.

Location tracking can be used by apps to provide valuable services like map navigation. But sometimes their activities are not what you'd expect. For example, the Spanish Premier Football League phone app used location tracking to identify football fans in bars and then turned on their microphones to record and identify bars that were showing football games without a valid licence. This unlawful activity earned the football league a $280,000 fine for a breach of GDPR law[71].

Your phone apps don't just exploit your phone data for their own purposes. Most apps also share your data with third parties. For example, 61% of phone apps tested by Privacy International transmitted personal data to Facebook[72] - including dating apps and health apps. Most apps are free precisely because they share your data with advertisers.

In China, it's now mandatory for all mobile phone users to turn on facial recognition so they can be personally identified by the State each time they use their phones.[73]

The mobile phone market is dominated by Google Android devices with 72% market share and Apple iPhone with 27%[74]. Whether this is a monopoly market or a duopoly market is open to debate.

As with laptops, there are no mainstream phone manufacturers that offer privacy by design. Niche players include the company Blackphone which targets corporate customers. Recent market entrants for the very early adopter market include Purism's Librem 5 and the more cost effective PinePhone from the PINE64 community. Both phones run Linux operating systems including the Ubuntu Touch mobile OS.

Another option for your existing Android phone is to install an alternative Android operating system that does not include Google proprietary code – or necessitate the use of Google Play store for apps. LineageOS is one of the more mature examples but it is not for the technically unadventurous - and its avoidance of using Google Play Store in favour of F-Droid apps presents a number of challenges for average users.

Which leaves the iPhone versus regular Android phones. Research has shown that iPhones share 10x less data than Android phones[75]. This is no doubt because of Google's advertising revenue business model versus Apple's hardware sales model – 'you the product' versus 'you the customer'. As such, the only mainstream choice for a relatively privacy-oriented phone is the Apple iPhone.... until Linux phones go mainstream that is.

# Digital Privacy Self-defence

Some quick tips for phone privacy & security:

- Set a strong, alphanumeric password so data on lost phones is protected
- Disable notification previews for when your phone is unattended
- Disable GPS for when you don't need it for maps and navigation
- Beware that photos taken by your phone will include data about your phone and possibly location.
- Using webapps than run in your browser rather than Google Play store apps can protect more of your data.

Also beware of any applications that may be uploading your unencrypted messages or data to the cloud – as WhatsApp was discovered doing[76].

It's worth taking the time to go through each of your app permissions and turn off anything that looks unnecessary or anything you're uncomfortable with sharing. You'll know if something was essential if the app stops working.

# Smart devices: The Internet of Things

Smart devices are basically computerised objects with sensors such as thermometers, microphones or cameras. They usually connect to online services to enable their purpose – such as storing video footage. Collectively, these types of devices are known as the 'Internet of Things' ('IoT'). The IoT is on track to be considerably bigger than the current internet. It seems all devices aspire to be smart devices.

For 'smart' device, think 'surveillance' device.

Personal assistants such as Amazon Alexa or Google Assistant are probably the leading examples of smart devices. They make our lives easier and fun with voice commands and authoritative voice answers. But to enable this value proposition they must always listen to us, identify us and record us.

Many people find this a bit creepy – and in some professional contexts, such as lawyers working from home, unacceptable.

In 2019, Google and Amazon came out swinging in a legal case in the State of Illinois, USA - and successfully defended their right to turn on their devices at any time, without your consent[77]. It's unlikely this would stand up in a European court.

Another popular smart device is Amazon's Ring doorbell. Ring allows you to answer the doorbell using your phone, and record the comings and goings outside your house with its video camera and microphone.

The Amazon Ring marketing department had no concerns publishing cute footage of children Trick or Treating during Halloween in 2019[78]. This was enabled by the fact that all Ring customer video footage is stored on Amazon's services. Ring has become with a valuable resource for both US and UK law enforcement. They've been co-opted by Amazon to actively market the devices to residents[79] – and have shared live and recorded videos with the police without warrants or consent[80].

In 2021 Amazon turned on Amazon Sidewalk - a neighbourhood wireless network created by devices like Amazon Echo, Ring security cams, outdoor lights, motion sensors, and tile trackers. This 'mesh' network connects your devices with your neighbours by default - it is an opt-out service - and has a range of up to one mile. Amazon can track any Sidewalk-enabled device passing through a 'Sidewalk neighbourhood'. For example, Amazon could know that a user walked by a house, unlocked a nearby door or found a lost item in a nearby street, and when[81].

Google Nest is another popular smart device that enables you to control your home thermostat from your phone. Data from the device is shared with Google. In 2019 it was discovered that Google Nest also contained a hidden, undisclosed microphone.[82]

The UK has seen a big push for the adoption of smart meters in the last five years. Smart meters monitor your household's energy consumption and enable specific devices to be identified by their energy profile. In 2022, the UK Government announced plans to collect all smart meter data into a central government database[83]. In the US, the appeals court has ruled that energy consumption data collected by smart meters is protected by the Fourth Amendment, which prohibits unreasonable searches and seizures[84].

Televisions too are increasingly becoming smart, with a built-in ability to monitor rooms and respond to voice commands. The FBI has warned US citizens to cover TV cameras to protect their privacy[85].

Fitness trackers are smart devices that monitor our sporting activity or lack thereof - including a users weight, birth date, photos, GPS coordinates, heart rate, steps and social data. They've proved to be less fit in terms of compliance with privacy regulations[86] - and Google's acquisition of Fitbit in 2021 has raised privacy concerns.

Games consoles are now smart for your children - and you should expect that they are watching, listening and recording unless you know otherwise.[87]

In 2019, Mercedes was in the headlines for covertly tracking the movements of its new cars[88]. The automotive industry seems to be claiming the right to the data that your car produces[89].

Tesla[90] and some other manufacturers now have internal facing 'cabin' cameras with microphones in their cars. You should take appropriate steps to protect the privacy of yourself and your passengers if needed.

Other smart devices to watch out for include smart clothes, smart white goods, smart beds and smart employee trackers.

Smart devices are also at considerable risk from hackers. Each smart device is like a mini-computer but unlike computers they rarely get security updates – assuming they even had adequate security in the first place. And the way smart devices store data in the cloud may also be insecure.

Children are not immune to the proliferation of smart devices. In 2017, a children's "CloudToy" teddy bear, manufactured by US company Spiral Toys, came to market that allowed young children and their parents to exchange personal messages. It left two million recorded messages exposed online for anyone to see and listen to and was subsequently held to ransom by hackers[91].

In 2015, the children's doll 'My Friend Kayla', manufactured by US company Genesis Toys, that listened to your child to learn what they like and don't like, was banned by authorities in Germany for being a spy device – as was a similar doll dubbed by the German press as the 'Stasi-Barbie'[92]. These devices were found by security researchers to be easy to hack such that hackers could engage in a dialogue with the child directly through the toys.

Kids smart trackers, designed for parents to monitor a child's location, are regularly found to lack basic security from being hacked[93].

And even smart adult toys can be sharing intimate data and be vulnerable to hackers[94].

Medical implants are also becoming smart – allowing remote access for doctors and software updates. A security vulnerability in a smart pacemaker that had been implanted in 500,000 patients lead to an urgent recall in 2017 as it was feared that hackers could increase or decrease heart rates at will[95].

# Digital Privacy Self-defence

Here are a few things to consider when buying a smart device:

- Search for stories of the device being hacked before you buy
- Check the privacy policy
- Will your data be shared with third parties?
- How can your data be deleted?
- What legal jurisdiction applies?
- Check if software updates are enabled and for how long
- Check if you will be alerted if the device is hacked
- Can the microphone and camera can be turned off?

Another smart device privacy tip worth following: When staying in holiday accommodation, check the room for hidden cameras with a quick network device scan using the smartphone app Fing.

And consider domestic abuse threats with regards to smart devices. If you don't have control of smart devices within your home you could become vulnerable to others.

# Smart cities

Cities are now getting smart. Internet of Things devices are increasingly collecting data on us as we go about our daily lives, so that authorities can provide enhanced public services – and public security services in particular. In the context of privacy, smart cities can be considered as surveillance cities.

London is a global leader in citizen surveillance, coming in at number 6 in the top CCTV surveilled cities in the world, with numbers 1-5 in China[96]. Despite the considerable expenditure and threat to civil liberties, evidence for the correlation between the number of public CCTV cameras and crime or safety levels is mixed.

In 2016 the Metropolitan police in London began a three year trial of live facial recognition ('LFR') cameras on public crowds with the goal of catching known criminals. These have been heavily criticised by privacy advocates who have questioned the legal basis and efficacy given the human rights risks and only handful of arrests. Despite ongoing legal challenges, in 2020 the decision was taken to roll out LFR across London[97].

Indeed, the UK government had already signed a £300m contract with the US defence contractor Leidos in 2019 for the provision of a UK national facial recognition system[98] – with oversight from the Surveillance Camera Commissioner and his "National Surveillance Camera Strategy"[99].

Surveillance cameras are big business. Big revenue for the security industry selling them but also big revenue for local authorities that make millions from traffic offence fines. In London, over half a million pounds in fines are automatically generated every day.[100]

Automated Number Plate Recognition ('ANPR') that links your identity to your vehicle is also becoming widespread for both commercial use, such as in car parks, and by law enforcement agencies.

# Securing networks

The way in which you connect to the internet is a key area of risk for digital privacy.

In 2019 Google was taken to court for wiretapping. It had used its Google Streetmap cars to collect Wi-Fi data from millions of people's houses around the world. The US Supreme Court stated that Wi-Fi surveillance did fall under US wiretapping law. However, Google somehow avoided billions of dollars in fines and settled the case out of court for $13m - approximately 4 minutes worth of Google's profit[101].

Securing your home Wi-Fi is important for security and privacy. Anyone with a moderate interest in hacking can download the hackers operating system, Kali Linux, for free and use its built-in tools to hack into your Wi-Fi. And they can do so from the comfort of 300 metres away if they spend £20 on a bigger antenna. It may surprise you to learn that the amateur world record for picking up a Wi-Fi signal at ground level is 237 miles[102].

You can access the security settings of your home Wi-Fi router using your web browser. Just enter the common router IP address of 192.168.1.1 (or sometimes your manufacturer has an alternative IP address for its device). It's best to do this with a direct Ethernet cable connection to your router if possible.

Be sure to change the username and password, as the defaults for most brands are known to hackers Also change your network name (the SSID) from the default, which will often indicate your ISP or router brand. And be sure to check and update your firmware (the software) for your router. Updating will not normally change your settings.

While you're at it, if you have children, and wish to time limit their internet access, you can also assign a fixed 'MAC address' to each of their devices and set access time slots for each day of the week.

When using a Wi-Fi outside your home, in a cafe for instance, make sure you're connecting to their official network name. A fake Wi-Fi signal can be created by anyone with a nearby laptop and a reasonably priced 'pineapple' device.

Also, try to get into the habit of turning off your mobile phone's Wi-Fi and Bluetooth when you're not using them. Beacons in shops and street furniture devices have the ability to track your phone movements as you go about your business, and perhaps identify you as their online customer[103].

# VPNs & Tor Browser

To protect your online activity when you're connected to the internet you can use a Virtual Private Network services ('VPN') and the Tor web browser.

One of the main ways to identify you when you go online is via your Internet Protocol ('IP') address. An IP address is a unique number identifier attributed to every device that connects to the internet. When your laptop connects to the internet your ISP assigns you an IP address. This is usually on a per household basis and does not normally change.

When you visit a website, the website records your IP address. If you have an account with the website, it can link your IP address to your personal details. As you surf the internet, ad networks and web services can track your IP address across websites you visit.

Your IP address will also reveal your location , with varying levels of accuracy. If you visit whatsmyipaddress.com you'll see your IP address and its location. Often, it will actually be the location of your ISP, but country and city level are usually accurate.

IP addresses which are allocated on a household basis can be a challenge for online adverts and web personalisations designed to target individuals. It's not uncommon for your internet activity to be confused with other members of your household and for them to be shown adverts or personalised recommendations or search results based on your online activity, or vice-versa. This may cause problems for you if you were researching a surprise birthday present or symptoms of a disease, for example.

When you connect to the internet, an unencrypted connection will be visible to anyone recording or monitoring your activity, including your ISP. An encrypted connection between you and a website will be indicated by a closed padlock to the left of your browser address bar. This indicates a secure HTTPS connection rather than an insecure, unencrypted HTTP connection. Most websites are now HTTPS by default but many are not.

Just like a laptop needs an IP address, websites also need an IP address. Your laptop and website communicate using these IP addresses to send you a web page or receive an upload for example.

IP addresses work well for devices talking to each other but they are not so good for humans who would rather type www.amazon.com than a string of IP address numbers like 96.127.3.17. As such, we have the Domain Name System ('DNS') which allocates readable domain names to IP addresses. When you type a web address into your web browser, the domain name is converted into an IP address in the background by the DNS system.

Your ISP will run a DNS server for this conversion purpose and if the ISP's DNS requests are unencrypted, which they often are, your ISP – and anyone else monitoring - will be able to record the domain names of all the websites you visit, even if the content of the web pages are encrypted with HTTPS.

A virtual private network service (VPN) can be used to prevent ISPs tracking and monitoring your internet activity. VPNs form an encrypted tunnel between your device and the VPNs server which then connects you to the internet. This usually includes encrypting DNS requests.

When using a VPN, your ISP knows you've connected to the VPN but they have no insight into what you are doing over that connection. This is particularly beneficial as a counter to mass government surveillance or to having your ISP data sold to advertisers - which is legal in the US but not in the EU.

Another primary benefit of a VPN is that it will allocate an IP address to your internet activity that is different from your home IP address - and so cannot be easily attributed to you or your location by a website. For example, some people use VPNs to access online services that are not available in their own country. VPNs are also good to use over untrusted networks, like free Wi-Fi in a cafe, so that all your online traffic is encrypted.

However, VPNs are by no means designed for online privacy. They effectively act as a hopefully more trusted replacement for your ISP and, as such, could technically see what you're doing online if they wanted to. If total anonymity is important to you it's also hard to avoid a money trail when buying a VPN service that does not point to your real identity, unless your VPN service accepts Bitcoin payments.

The problem with VPNs is that we must trust them not to be monitoring our online activities i.e. carrying out 'man-in-the-middle' attacks, as they are known. Many VPNs brand themselves as privacy services and are able to tick the boxes of what one might look for technically with regards privacy but this is hard to verify. They also are often headquartered in countries with less than stellar privacy protection or legal enforcement.

Proton VPN, HQ in Switzerland, is possibly the best all-round privacy proposition. It does not keep logs of your internet activity and Switzerland has strong privacy laws. However, always search for news on any privacy or security breaches before signing up for any specific VPN service.

Anonymity is the best form of privacy and Tor is designed for anonymous online activity. Tor is a global network of routers set-up and maintained by independent tech-savvy Tor supporters.

Tor servers provide encrypted internet access when you use the Tor web browser. The network protects your privacy and anonymity by routing your activities via three routers to ensure that no one router knows the start or destination of the request. Like VPNs, your home IP address is anonymised in the process. Unlike VPNs, 'man-in-the-middle' monitoring is not possible; and there is no money trail back to you as the service is free.

You can download the Tor browser from torproject.org. Browsing is occasionally slower than normal and you may find that some websites block you or are dysfunctional, but on the whole, the Tor browsing experience is very good.

Documents published by Edward Snowden revealed that the US National Security Agency is not a fan of Tor as it's next to impossible for them to spy on[104]. China blocks Tor for the same reason. And Russia is now trying to do the same[105].

As well as being able to view most normal websites, the Tor browser can view 'onion sites' that are anonymously hosted on the Tor network itself. This is where the infamous 'dark web' can be found - a place where content, communication and commerce can occur away from the prying eyes of state surveillance. This is useful if you live under an oppressive government regime but is also a tool for criminal behaviour.

In reality, onion sites are as much a place of enlightenment as they are of shady dealings. For example, using Tor you can find:

- Riseup: a volunteer-run email provider for political activists
- Sci-Hub: a platform for over 50 million free science research papers
- ProPublic: the first online publication that won a Pulitzer Prize
- The BBC
- Facebook

To double-down on your online privacy - and anonymity - you can first connect to your VPN and then connect to Tor. This is called 'nesting'. And the secure HTTPS web browser connection will give you a third layer of protection.

# Web browsing threats

Beyond network threats, everyday web browsing will threaten your privacy in many ways.

Web cookies are the most infamous problem. These are small files that websites leave in your web browser. Cookies are often necessary for website personalisation, such as remembering what's in your shopping cart. However, they are also commonly used for marketing purposes such as following you around the internet with an advert for a product that you've viewed but not bought - 're-targeting' as online marketers call it.

Website cookies can be 'first party' i.e. placed by the website itself; or 'third party' i.e. placed by an entity other than the website but with a presence on the web page such as the advertising networks or web services mentioned previously. Under the EU's General Data Protection Regulations cookies are personally identifiable information and require your consent – hence the annoying and omnipresent cookie permission pop-ups.

Third party cookies are particularly problematic when you visit sensitive content. For example, in 2020 the Mayo Clinic's HIV testing service was using cookies from Google, Microsoft Bing and others, all of whom may recognise you from your IP address or your login cookies from their services.

Another privacy threat is using browsers like Google's Chrome that comes with an attributed advertising ID and links your account with your web browsing history[106].

'Browser fingerprinting' is a particular problem. It's a highly accurate way of identifying you based on the unique characteristics of your web browser and operating system. This data is usually automatically shared when you visit a website. Google's terms and conditions actually specify that Google will use this technique to identify you.

Some browsers, like Firefox, will block browser fingerprinting requests. Using Tor browser is also a good protection against being fingerprinted, as Tor browsers all look the same if you follow their recommendation to not change the browser in any way, such as adding new plug-ins.

In terms of desktop web browser market share, Google is the winner with its Chrome browser at 63% market share; Microsoft Edge is at 10%; Apple's Safari at 10%; and Mozilla's Firefox at 7%[107].

So, which browser is best for digital privacy? Once again the application with a low market share comes out on top: Firefox.

- Firefox is free and open source software
- It gives you full access to its privacy-related settings
- It is run by a not-for-profit company, Mozilla

Although ironically, Mozilla makes most of its money from Google paying to be Firefox's default search engine.

Brave browser is also worth considering as a good solution that does not require customisation or add-ons to give a good privacy experience.

# Web browser settings

Using Firefox as your primary web browser, which you can do on your laptop and on your phone, is a great start in improving your online privacy compared to other web browsers. However, there's work to be done to customise Firefox's settings to maximise your privacy.

Let's start with the basic settings in Firefox's Preferences menu.

Set the Homepage and New Tabs to blank to prevent 3rd party content getting loaded each time you use Firefox. Next, remove all content from being displayed on the home page.

Moving on to Search preferences:

Google search has a monopoly on the search market with 93% market share, with Microsoft's Bing and Verizon's Yahoo each at around 2%.

Given Google's goal of acquiring and monetising as much data about you as possible, it's clearly not the best choice for your digital privacy.

Probably the best search engine for privacy today is Qwant.com. Qwant launched in 2013 with its HQ in Paris, France. It's one of the few EU-based search engines and has its own indexing engine. It claims not to employ user tracking and doesn't personalize search results in order to avoid trapping users in a filter bubble. Being French, it falls under strong EU data protection laws and outside of the government data collection powers of the US Cloud Act 2018.

To add Qwant to your Firefox search engine list visit Qwant.com, click on the three dots on the right side of the web address bar, and select 'Add Search Engine'. It's worth noting that you have the option in Qwant's Settings on the Qwant website to turn on or off adult content filtering, news stories and social media results.

In your Firefox Search preferences uncheck 'Provide search suggestions' and delete all search engines other than Qwant, which you can add as your default search engine.

Should Qwant fail to provide adequate results for any reason you may also wish to add another privacy-centric search engine like StartPage.com as. It actually uses Google's search results but acts as a proxy in-between you and Google so that Google does not identify you. StartPage HQ is in the Netherlands. Try them both out and set the best one as default.

DuckDuckGo.com is a credible, privacy-focused search engine but due to being subject to the US Cloud Act 2018 it cannot attain the highest level of privacy.

Moving on to Firefox's Privacy and Security settings, choose Custom and only select Fingerprinters. Other settings will be dealt with later by the add-on 'uBlock Origin'.

I would suggest deleting cookies and site data when Firefox closes to protect the privacy and security of your laptop. and minimise unwanted tracking and browser compromise risks.

For the same reason never save passwords and logins in your browser. This is an inconvenience when you restart your browser and have to re-enter logins but is security and privacy best practice. For the same reason it is best not to create a web browser account.

A quick word on the 'private browsing' function of your web browser: Private browsing does not keep your online activities private from your ISP or from the websites that you visit... but it does prevent history and website data from being remembered on your laptop. It's also useful to use temporarily when using someone else's device for logging-in to your accounts.

To complete your privacy settings, don't share usage data with Firefox or allow it to install studies.

Don't block dangerous content as this service shares data on the websites that you visit with Mozilla and / or Google. And don't query OCSP responder servers for the same reason, it is a service of no benefit.

Once you've been through the Firefox Preferences settings it's time to dig deeper and make some changes to the Firefox configuration settings. These can be access by typing about:config in the browser web address bar and accepting the risk warning. Key settings to check and amend – which you can find by typing in the 'Search preference bar' include:

*browser.safebrowsing.malware.enabled*
Double click to set to false to disable sharing your website data with Mozilla / Google.

*dom.battery.enabled = false*
Set to false to stop website owners tracking the battery status of your device as an ID mechanism.

*dom.event.clipboardevents.enabled*
Set to false to disable websites getting notifications of what you copy, paste or cut.

*media.navigator.enabled*
Set to false to prevent websites tracking your microphone and camera status.

*network.dns.disablePrefetch*
Set to true to disable pre-fetching of links on a page that you haven't even clicked on yet.

*network.http.referer.trimmingPolicy = 2*
Set to 2 to restrict information about the website you came from being shared with the website you are currently on.

Changing your Firefox configuration settings can cause functional problems on some websites. It's worth having a back-up web browser installed, such as Brave, to use when such issues occur.

# Web browser Add-ons

Web browser add-ons should be used to add further privacy hardening to Firefox. These can be found in your Firefox preferences under 'Add-ons / Find more extensions'. All the suggested add-ons are free and open source software.

uBlock Origin is an extension that gives you the means to block adverts, cookies, trackers and even unwanted content. By blocking adverts, pages are easier to navigate and load much faster.

uBlock Origin works by using publicly available filter lists of know ad networks and web services. When you visit a website uBlock references the list locally and blocks those elements on the web page – all in a fraction of a second.

You can see and change these lists by clicking on the uBlock shield icon on your web browser, selecting preferences and selecting 'I am an advanced user' – then clicking on the Filter list tabs. The more lists you add the more blocking that occurs.

The default settings when you install uBlock Origin do a good job at protecting your privacy and if you're not a dabbler you need do no more.

However, declaring yourself an 'advanced user' in the settings gives you the ability to make custom edits to your blocking preferences. When you visit a website you can click on the uBlock shield icon and see a list of the cookies, trackers and web services that have been blocked, partially blocked or not blocked – indicated in the far left column by red for blocked, amber for partially blocked and green for not blocked. To the right of the element's name are a further two columns.

The left column is for custom settings that will apply to every website you visit. The column to the far right is for only the website you are on.

uBlock Origin is one of the most important tools in your digital privacy self-defence and it's well worth watching some YouTube videos on the subject to upskill your capabilities.
Using uBlock Origin can cause functional problems on some websites. If the problem cannot be fixed by allowing some blocked cookies to function, you may need to turn off uBlock Origin for that website. If that doesn't work, use a back-up web browser, such as Brave. Privacy is inevitably a game of compromise.

When you're using uBlock Origin, you may wish to buy a subscription to your favourite websites that rely on advertising revenue for their survival.

Our next add-on is Multi-Account Containers. Without containers, if you signed into Google's Gmail in a browser tab and then open Google Maps in a new browser tab you'd automatically be signed-in to your Google account in Maps i.e. Google Maps will know who you are even if you hadn't wanted it to.

However, with Containers installed you can set up a container for Gmail and a separate container for Google Maps. Maps would then be unable to identify you unless you specifically signed into Maps, even though you had previously signed in to Gmail. By using Containers, Google can be prevented from identifying you when you're on non-Google websites that contain Google advertising or Google web services, which is most websites.

You should set-up separate containers for all the major websites you log into to prevent them using off-site tracking too.

# Websites & Social media

When you visit a website, your use of that website is governed by its Terms & Conditions and its Privacy Policy. Given these are often long and difficult to read I recommend instead looking at the aptly named website 'Terms of service didn't read' website[108]. Here you'll find an easy-to-read legal summary for the most popular websites.

You should review your online account privacy options regularly, as options are liable to change without notice. Perhaps set yourself a 6-monthly calendar reminder.

Your Google account settings are also worth your time and attention. For example, Google now compiles a list of the products you've bought based on what it knows about you from Gmail and other sources. And everywhere you've ever been is tracked by Google Maps unless you advise it otherwise. These may or may not be a positive value proposition for you.

Another thing to look out for is being tracked even after you log out of a website. This is done by Big Tech companies that have reach across the internet with multiple brands, advertising networks or web services. For example, someone who hadn't logged into Facebook for years but had failed to turn off "Off-Facebook Activity" in their Facebook account settings would subsequently be able to view a lot of their internet activity history in their Facebook account[109]. LinkedIn, which is owned by Microsoft, has a similar off-site tracking setting you should turn off.

As discussed, uBlock Origin and Firefox Containers are your friends when it comes to blocking such tracking activity.

With websites generally, the name of the game is to minimise sharing your data – which is something the website owner should also be doing from a GDPR compliance perspective. With some web services you'll find it important to take account of what country's law applies in their Terms & Conditions to assess the privacy risks.

It's best not to let websites remember your credit card details given the continuous risk from hackers.

In particular, avoid revealing very personal details like your mother's maiden name that might be used to access your more valuable, high security services, like online bank accounts. Just because a website asks for a maiden name doesn't mean you have to supply the correct one.

Pay particular attention not to sign up for unwanted marketing communications.

And finally, diversify as much as possible the websites and services you use to minimise single vendor profiling.

You may wish to consider using decentralised social media services such as Mastodon or diaspora. These are privacy-friendly and have most of the features of Big Tech social networks. If you can convince a small group of friends to switch, others will follow. The network effect.

# Office applications

Google's G Suite and Microsoft's Office 365 dominate the cloud office suite market. However, a free and open source alternative to some of the cloud applications is Nextcloud, which you can even host on your own cloud server. It is used by many governments and enterprises.

As a better privacy alternative to the cloud for the more tech savvy, you could host a server in your own home such as the small tech company OpenProducts.com KEEP device (disclosure: I've worked with OpenProducts). It plugs into your Wi-Fi router and includes Nextcloud and an email server. All the software is free and open source and so is the hardware.

For a fully decentralise file back-up service that runs on your laptop and not in the cloud look no further than Storj.io. Storj encrypts your files locally then distributes multiple copies of them across its secure network of thousands of member computers.

Or you may wish to back-up your data to a local hard drive and store it in a fireproof safe in your home. Back-up your back-up to mitigate against hardware failure.

For a non-cloud free and open source office suite try the popular LibreOffice.org suite. It's compatible with Microsoft file formats and includes the equivalent of Word, Excel and PowerPoint. This book was created on LibreOffice Writer.

There are free and open source alternatives to most popular computer applications that run on Mac, Windows and Linux.

# Email & Messaging

In terms of privacy, email is best regarded as sending a postcard. There are numerous stages in the life of an email where it is unencrypted – often by default - and therefore insecure and not private. If you use a popular web-based email service like Gmail, Microsoft Outlook, or Yahoo! Mail your emails can be scanned and read by those companies. Most popular email services sell advertising based on what they know about you.

Email is easy to fake or 'spoof' and hard to verify when necessary. You can send your friends fake emails that look like they are coming from any company you wish using online services.

ProtonMail is possibly the most well known private email service. Protonmail is a subscription service and does not require any user data for the purposes of selling advertising. It uses end-to-end (E2EE) email encryption and is unable to read emails sent between Protonmail users. When sending to non-Protonmail users (Gmail, Microsoft, etc.), emails are not E2EE by default (so not private) but they can be made encrypted for pick-up by the recipient on the Protonmail site without a Protonmail account. It's based in Switzerland which has robust privacy laws.

With regards to email, privacy by compartmentalisation, for example not using an email service supplied by your preferred search engine, helps increase your privacy.

The best way to ensure secure and private conversations either 1-on-1 or in groups is to use an end-to-end encrypted messaging app. Signal app, created by the not-for-profit Signal Foundation, is the most secure messaging app. Unlike WhatsApp, it's fully free and open source - and encrypts your meta data (who / when) as well as your message content. Signal has been audited by third party security professionals. Signal can also be used for voice calls and video chats with the same level of security and privacy.

# Passwords

Well known websites are regularly in the news for being hacked and suffering major breaches of data. As such, you should expect that your personal data will be in the hands of a hacker sometime soon.

In fact, you can check if your email address has been part of a data breach already by entering it on the website HaveIBeenpwned.com (poned meaning 'owned'). The service, created by security expert Troy Hunt in 2013, collects and analyses hundreds of database dumps and pastes with information about billions of leaked accounts. I'm reasonably confident that you'll be there.

It's not just hackers we should worry about. In 2019 it was revealed that Facebook had stored 600 million passwords in plain text i.e. they were readable by any of their staff who had access[110].

A 2018 Cyber Security survey[111] revealed the shameful state of people's passwords in the UK: 123456 was used 23 million times; the word 'password' 3.6 million times; a variety of football club names; famous musicians; and fictional characters like 'superman' also proved very popular. On top of this, around 60% of us are using the same password every time we set up an online account.

Websites should not normally store your password in readable, plain text. Your passwords are usually converted into a string of unreadable characters using a one-way mathematical function.

This process is called 'hashing' and creates a 'hash code' of your password.

When a hacker steals a customer database, they need to crack the hash codes to reveal all the passwords. Hackers can use brute force to crack simple passwords up to 6-characters long within a reasonable amount of time and computational effort. Brute force attacks are when a computer tries every possible combination of letters and characters to find the matching hash.

Brute force is a hacker's least preferred option to use on a large database or longer passwords given the computing power and time required. Instead, hackers use existing lists of common password hashes - called 'rainbow tables' - to match the stolen hash codes to real passwords. They also use dictionary tables of common word hashes and common word combination hashes - including predictable permutations of words like replacing specific letters with numbers or symbols.

Using these widely available hacking techniques, a hacker could probably crack 50% of passwords in an average customer database in a matter of hours. Once a password has been cracked the hacker will be able to access your account on that site and any other sites where you've used the same password.

Cracking passwords is something that computers are particularly good at. The average computer with a 4GHz processor runs at 4 billion cycles per second. With a brute force attack the password 123456 would be cracked almost instantly. As you add length and complexity to a password the difficulty of cracking the hash of it climbs rapidly. For example, a 9-character password using only numbers took a computer (in 2012) 4-seconds to break... but a 9-character password with numbers, upper- and lower-case letters, and symbols, took the same computer 12-years to break.

So, it pays to have long and complex passwords that include numbers, letters and symbols. Particularly given that computing power continues to double approximately every 18-months, known as 'Moore's Law'.

Your passwords should be at least 12-characters in length. But how do you create one? Here's a useful technique. Firstly, think of a memorable sentence of at least 12 words. The more obscure and least related to things people know or could find out about you the better. Try to have more than one capitalised word. Next, take the first letter of each word. Then replace some of the letters with numbers and symbols. You will now have a secure password which common hacking techniques would find very hard to break. Next step is to create a unique password for every online account that you have – and remember them. To make this task a lot easier, we turn to password managers.

A password manager is a software program that creates and stores all your passwords. I recommend the free and open source KeePass.info. KeePass takes the hard work out of creating and remembering long and complex passwords for each website. Although you do need to remember your KeePass password or you'll lose access to all your passwords. Write it down and keep it in a hidden place just in case.

Each time you set-up an account on a website, open KeePass, create a new entry for the website and then have KeePass create a password that's 20 or more characters long. Just copy and paste the password into the account set up and do the same each time you need to log in. You won't know or remember what the password is and you don't need to.

To share your passwords with your phone, install the KeePass2 app and email yourself the password file from your laptop periodically. Your phone app can then automatically fill in your online passwords if you choose it to do so. The file also acts as a back up to your laptop file.

KeePass is a great way to keep track of all the sites you've registered with. Because all your passwords are unique and complex – and you never type them - it's probably not necessary to change them more than every couple of years as a hygiene factor.

Never use your web browser to save passwords as this is not sufficiently secure[112].

Another good practice to protect your security and privacy is to use 'two factor authentication' (2FA), supported by most websites and apps. 2FAonline services support 2FA uses two of either something you know like a password; something you have like a phone; or something you are like a fingerprint. Most bank apps use 2FA by sending a text message to your phone.

AndOTP is a free and open source app that you can use on your phone to generate two-factor authentication codes for websites.

# Deleting data

When you dispose of your laptop it's important to fully remove your data to protect your privacy and security.

Normally, when you delete a file, the file remains on your hard drive but disappears from your file system. The file will be over-written if your laptop needs the space. This means that files which have been deleted and not yet over-written can easily be recovered using readily available software.

To fully erase files from your system you can use CCleaner for Windows and Mac; or a number of free and open source applications for Linux. These applications over-write all areas of your hard-drive that are marked free and therefore destroy any previously deleted files. Only one pass is required to be effective.

Another way to ensure your privacy is not compromised when disposing of your laptop – and something already recommended to mitigate a theft, is to fully encrypt your hard drive.

When it comes to disposal time, re-install your operating system or do a full factory reset. The new owner could certainly try to recover your data but because they don't have your encryption password, any hard drive data would be encrypted nonsense.

In most circumstances, the GDPR legislation will compel a website to delete your data if you make a request for it to do so. However, you should be aware that people trying to have their DNA data deleted from online testing services have discovered a lot of legal loopholes[113]. In the US, judges are now authorising access to online DNA test data to law enforcement agencies[114]. You might want to think twice before using such services, for the protection of yourself and all your family members.

# Legal action

Having some understanding of the law that relates to your privacy and personal data protection rights is very useful when deciding which online services to use. It's also useful should you get into a dispute with a website owner; or indeed should you wish to take legal action to seek compensation for material damage or distress.

The key pieces of UK legislation that relate to privacy and personal data protection are the Data Protection Act 2018 (DPA 2018) which incorporates the EU's General Data Protection Regulations of 2018; and the Privacy and Electronic Communications Regulations 2003 (PECR).

A good source of consumer friendly information about your digital rights is the UK's Information Commissioner's Office website. Here you'll be pleased to learn that the DPA 2018 gives you:

- the right to be informed about data use
- the right to access your data
- the right to rectification of wrong data
- the right to restrict processing to the original intended process
- the right to portability of your data
- the right to object against processing
- the right to an explanation of how automated, algorithmic processes have made a personal decision about you; and
- the right to be notified of any data breaches

These rights apply to all EU citizens regardless of whether the website is in the EU or not.

The key take away from PECR is that you may only be marketed to with your explicit consent. You must opt-in rather than having to opt-out.

It's also worth knowing that the DPA 2018 obligates digital businesses to comply with its principals of data protection by design and by default. If the people, processes or technology in a business are not aligned around privacy protection then action can be taken by the Information Commissioner's Office.

And unlike previous UK data protection legislation the DPA 2018 has some teeth. As with GDPR, companies can be fined for infringements up to £17.5 million or 4% of annual global turnover, whichever is greater. Max Schrems, an Austrian lawyer and privacy activist, filed GDPR infringement cases totalling €3.9 billion against Google and Facebook on the first day GDPR came into force.

There'se been a steady stream of less ambitious cases in the UK courts. In the UK, British Airways has been fined €204 million and Marriott Hotels €110 million for DPA 2018 data breach infringements.

The climate is certainly favourable to legal action against Big Tech. Authorities in Germany, Sweden and the Netherlands have advised against using WhatsApp[115], Facebook and Microsoft's Office 365 on the basis that those services are incompatible with GDPR compliance.

In the US, Amazon is facing a class action law suit over the security breaches of its Ring doorbell system[116].

But Big Tech continues to fight against any privacy legislation that restricts its surveillance business models. Competing against the half-a-billion dollars they've spent on lobbying politicians in the last decade is an uphill struggle for voters[117].

# Political action

The threats to our digital privacy require politicians to not only understand rapidly evolving technologies and their privacy implications but to prioritise our rights over Big Tech interests. As such, keeping abreast of new developments and sharing your primary concerns with your MP is time well spent. Groups that are actively fighting for your digital privacy like Liberty, Open Rights Group, Privacy International and Big Brother Watch also deserve your support and donations.

# Part 2 Summary

This concludes Part 2: How do we protect our digital privacy?

Part 2 covered the technical fundamentals without which digital services cannot protect our privacy, and how these fundamentals apply to personal devices. It looked at the privacy risks of smart devices and how they might be reduced... and how smart cities take away privacy at the state level. It looked at how to secure network connections, including VPNs and the Tor browser.

To protect web browsing privacy, it covered privacy hardening Firefox and its add-ons... and how to secure websites, social media and office applications. It reviewed the inherent insecurity of email and its alternatives; how passwords can be made both stronger and easier; and how data history can be erased.

And finally, where technical measures fall short, it looked at the opportunity for legal action; and where legal powers fall short, political action.

# Part 3: The Future of Digital Privacy

# Digital Privacy Self-defence

*"There is another world, but it is in this one."*
W.B. Yeats

To fully safeguard every individual's digital privacy in the future, digital services will need to be decentralised, encrypted, and run on free and open source software.

It's likely that decentralised services will remain harder to build, harder to fund, harder to commercialise and harder to take to market than centralised services. The business opportunity for entrepreneurs and investors is relatively weak, unless new market verticals can be rapidly exploited. Equally, the privacy advantage for consumers is unlikely to prove sufficient to ensure mass market take up of a new service without also having a functional or price benefit that is an order of magnitude better than centralised competitors.

Blockchain has so far proved to be an infertile platform for mass market decentralised innovations, despite the trend for crypto-currency monetisation using Initial Coin Offerings ('ICO'). The leading crypt-currency, Bitcoin, also shows no sign of replacing fiat currency and fulfilling its promise of privacy and freedom from government monetary controls.

However, governments around the world are now reviewing the crypto-currency opportunity to replace their fiat currencies with Central Bank Digital Currency ('CBDC')[118]. CBDC is a centralised, official, government-issued digital currency that would enable the government to monitor all money transactions and create rules on how individuals can spend money. It replaces all cash. For example, the government could restrict an individual from buying petrol if their carbon credits had been exceeded that month.

CBDC would allow total financial surveillance and mark the end of privacy as we known it. It will be hard for governments to resist the power gained from introducing CBDC – just as its been hard for them to resist partnering with Big Tech to nudge citizens.

Can encryption survive and thrive? As a ubiquitous necessity for security, it's hard to envisage that governments will agree to break encryption with their proposed back-door keys, but such moves are indeed afoot. If they succeed, for everyone but those that are willing to break the law to preserve human rights, there would be no digital privacy.

Can free and open source software continue to thrive? FOSS is widely embedded in the technology ecosystem today. It's likely to remain so, at least in the near future, as its value proposition aligns well with business's needs for keeping costs low, legal liabilities minimal and performance strong. Privacy and freedom is more of a fringe benefit for the majority of FOSS end users. The biggest privacy threat to FOSS is its displacement by software-as-a-service solutions which are centralised and not private by nature.

Given the above, it's hard to envisage a future mass migration of people from free, centralised, pseudo-encrypted, proprietary Big Tech platforms to paid-for, decentralised, encrypted, and FOSS privacy-respecting alternatives.

Governments seem equally disinclined or unable to systemically reduce the power of Big Tech. To quote Rick Falkvinge, founder of the Pirate Party & privacy advocate:

*"Privacy remains your own responsibility today. We all need to take it back merely by exercising our privacy rights, with whatever tools are at our disposal."* [119]

Looking further ahead, there's good reason to believe that the technologies we currently carry around with us will soon become a physical part of us. In the opinion of Professor Yuval Noah Harari, author of Sapiens & advisor to the World Economic Forum, "it will be the greatest evolution in biology since the appearance of life".

The 'transhumanists' that could afford to embed technologies such as Elon Musk's brain Neuralink[120], bionic eyes[121] robotic limbs[122] or blood nanobots[123] would elevate their knowledge, senses and physical capabilities to become 'God-like cyborgs'[124] - with dominion over humans. Mere humans could be nudged into being microchipped for improved control and productivity.[125]

Digital privacy self-defence would then require a more surgical approach, as Arnold Schwarzenegger's character 'Quaid' discovered in the futuristic movie Total Recall.

In his 2020 book "COVID-19: The Great Reset", Klaus Schwab, Founder and executive chairman of the World Economic Forum, considered the implications:

*"As the novelty of wearable tech gives way to necessity - and, later, as wearable tech becomes embedded tech - will we be deprived of the chance to pause, reflect, and engage in meaningful, substantive conversations? How will our inner lives and ties to those around us change?"*

In other words, what is left of our humanity if privacy is finally taken away?

It's not inconceivable that somewhere in the future Big Tech may look to increase shareholder value by supplying a digital democracy solution – on a global basis. In 2017 Facebook filed a patent for a 'political platform'[126]. However, if Big Tech power aligns with the rise of authoritarian political power, it could well create the most oppressive global regime the world has ever seen. UK Prime Minister Boris Johnson's 2019 speech to UN stated as much:

*"Digital authoritarianism is not, alas, the stuff of dystopian fantasy but of an emerging reality.... I believe governments have been simply caught unawares by the unintended consequences of the internet."[127]*

Under such a Big Tech authoritarianism, our security and compliance may no longer be managed by police but by algorithms judging our digital selves and drones nudging our physical selves. Charlie Brooker's Black Mirror[128] anthology made real.

Which begs the question: Should citizens mobilise to create a new bottom-up, decentralised, encrypted and open source democracy system – a new constitution if you like - to secure our future freedom? Perhaps the subject of another book.

# Nothing to hide?

As we draw to the end of our digital privacy journey, I hope that you not only have the knowledge and confidence to protect your own digital privacy but also the inspiration to share the issue of digital privacy with others. When you do, someone is sure to tell you that they have "nothing to hide". Maybe that's true. Maybe.

... but in the words of Edward Snowden:

*'Arguing that you don't care about the right to privacy because you have nothing to hide is no different than saying you don't care about free speech because you have nothing to say.'*

Privacy is our inalienable human right. Our right to decide who we share with. And like all human rights, if we take the steps to protect ourselves and those we care for, we can all live a good life.

# Notes

[1] Base: Data privacy: what a consumer really thinks 2015 - Percentage who consider data privacy to be a 'significant concern' 79%; (1000 UK adults); Big Brother Watch 2015 - Percentage concerned about personal privacy online 79% (1000)

[2] Research by security company RSA 2018

[3] BCG Global Consumer Sentiment Survey 2013 "How private do you consider the following types of personal data?"

[4] https://www.nbcnews.com/tech/tech-news/zuckerberg-demolish-30m-real-estate-keep-things-private-n580216

[5] https://www.legislation.gov.uk/ukpga/1998/42/schedule/1/part/l/chapter/7

[6] https://en.wikipedia.org/wiki/Tim_Berners-Lee

[7] https://www.theguardian.com/technology/2017/apr/04/tim-berners-lee-online-privacy-interview-turing-award

[8] https://www.buzzfeednews.com/article/meghara/period-tracker-apps-facebook-maya-mia-fem

[9] https://cglife.com/blog/23andme-sold-your-genetic-data-to-gsk-personalized-medicine-ethics/

[10] https://www.theguardian.com/technology/2017/jul/27/facebook-free-basics-developing-markets

[11] https://www.irishmirror.ie/news/google-accused-spying-children-young-6941803

[12] https://www.bbc.co.uk/news/business-16713562

[13] https://www.propublica.org/article/google-has-quietly-dropped-ban-on-personally-identifiable-web-tracking

[14] https://www.wsj.com/articles/peter-thiel-competition-is-for-losers-1410535536

[15] https://www.visualcapitalist.com/top-100-most-valuable-brands-in-2022/

[16] https://lifehacker.com/how-to-download-all-of-wikipedia-onto-a-usb-flash-drive-1798453949

[17] Price Waterhouse Coopers technology moneytree 2018

[18] https://www.independent.co.uk/news/people/bono-s-group-has-made-more-money-from-facebook-investment-than-from-all-his-music-10480378.html

[19] https://theintercept.com/2016/04/14/in-undisclosed-cia-investments-social-media-mining-looms-large/

[20] https://companiesmarketcap.com/software/largest-software-companies-by-market-cap/

[21] https://www.statista.com/statistics/1035623/leading-mobile-app-ad-network-sdks-android/

[22] https://w3techs.com/technologies/details/ta-googleanalytics

[23] https://www.theguardian.com/technology/2018/mar/04/has-dopamine-got-us-hooked-on-tech-facebook-apps-addiction

[24] https://gizmodo.com/how-facebook-figures-out-everyone-youve-ever-met-1819822691

[25] https://www.wired.com/story/just-google-it-a-short-history-of-a-newfound-verb/

[26] https://www.theweek.co.uk/97653/children-have-1300-photos-of-themselves-posted-online-by-age-13

[27] https://www.mic.com/impact/obscure-app-has-scraped-3-billion-photos-to-use-for-facial-recognition-is-selling-its-services-to-law-enforcement-21714989

[28] https://www.dailymail.co.uk/news/article-7904287/Betting-firms-granted-access-database-28-

MILLION-children.html
29

https://www.telegraph.co.uk/technology/2017/07/03/google
s-deepmind-nhs-misused-patient-data-trial-watchdog-says/
30    https://www.theguardian.com/society/2019/dec/08/nhs-
gives-amazon-free-use-of-health-data-under-alexa-advice-
deal
31

https://www.technologyreview.com/2019/07/23/134090/you
re-very-easy-to-track-down-even-when-your-data-has-been-
anonymized/
32  https://www.visualcapitalist.com/dominance-google-and-
facebook-one-chart/
33

https://www.forbes.com/sites/thomasbrewster/2017/03/30/fc
c-privacy-rules-how-isps-will-actually-sell-your-data/
34

https://www.forbes.com/sites/kalevleetaru/2018/04/05/the-
data-brokers-so-powerful-even-facebook-bought-their-data-
but-they-got-me-wildly-wrong/
35        https://techcrunch.com/2019/09/04/mental-health-
websites-in-europe-found-sharing-user-data-for-ads/
36 https://www.bbc.co.uk/news/technology-51134738
37

https://www.ted.com/talks/jaron_lanier_how_we_need_to_r
emake_the_internet
38

https://www.theguardian.com/society/2010/sep/09/cameron-
nudge-unit-economic-behaviour
39      https://www.consumerreports.org/privacy/developers-
dont-know-what-their-apps-do-with-your-data-
a1055672912/

40
https://www.theregister.com/2012/04/04/google_recaptcha_street_view/

[41] https://www.cbsnews.com/news/what-are-you-sharing-when-you-sign-in-with-facebook-or-google/

[42] https://www.pcmag.com/news/four-companies-control-67-of-the-worlds-cloud-infrastructure

43
https://www.datacenterknowledge.com/archives/2017/03/03/here-are-the-submarine-cables-funded-by-cloud-giants

[44] https://www.lifewire.com/big-tech-seems-ready-to-conquer-space-5083908

[45] https://www.theguardian.com/uk/2013/jun/21/gchq-cables-secret-world-communications-nsa

[46] https://www.huffpost.com/entry/why-amazons-collaboration_b_4824854

[47] Study lead by Stanford University researcher Michael Bernstein 2013

48
https://www.buzzfeednews.com/article/laurenstrapagiel/tiktok-algorithim-racial-bias

[49] https://www.varsity.co.uk/science/13591

[50] https://www.theverge.com/2016/5/20/11721890/uber-surge-pricing-low-battery

[51] https://www.independent.co.uk/tech/facebook-s-new-patent-could-mean-you-are-denied-a-loan-because-of-your-friends-10482622.html

[52] https://www.prnewswire.com/news-releases/social-media-mistakes-that-could-cost-you-the-job-300198857.html

[53] https://www.newsweek.com/facebook-performed-psychology-experiment-thousands-users-without-telling-

them-256914

[54] https://www.nationalgeographic.com/science/article/a-61-million-person-experiment-on-facebook-shows-how-ads-and-friends-affect-our-voting-behaviour

[55] https://ca.childrenshealthdefense.org/corruption/robert-epstein-warns-against-big-tech-manipulation/

[56] https://www.nbcnews.com/news/us-news/google-tracked-his-bike-ride-past-burglarized-home-made-him-n1151761

[57] https://www.theverge.com/2019/3/1/18246297/china-transportation-people-banned-poor-social-credit-planes-trains-2018

[58] https://www.theguardian.com/commentisfree/2016/feb/21/death-from-above-nia-csa-skynet-algorithm-drones-pakistan

[59] https://www.newscientist.com/article/2166207-discriminating-algorithms-5-times-ai-showed-prejudice/

[60] https://www.amnesty.org.uk/which-countries-access-your-data-nsa-gchq-five-eyes-snowden-surveillance

[61] https://www.theguardian.com/world/2013/jun/06/us-tech-giants-nsa-data

[62] https://www.channel4.com/news/gchq-nsa-broke-law-surveillance-prism-snowdown

[63] https://www.washingtonpost.com/news/wonk/wp/2016/04/27/new-study-snowdens-disclosures-about-nsa-spying-had-a-scary-effect-on-free-speech/

[64] https://www.bbc.co.uk/news/technology-31816410

[65] https://www.amnesty.org/en/latest/press-release/2019/11/google-facebook-surveillance-privacy/

[66] https://techcrunch.com/2018/12/05/australia-rushes-its-dangerous-anti-encryption-bill-into-parliament/

[67] https://www.informationweek.com/it-life/online-security-

how-the-experts-keep-safe

68 https://gs.statcounter.com/os-market-share/desktop/worldwide

69 https://www.cbsnews.com/video/60-minutes-shows-how-easily-your-phone-can-be-hacked/

70

https://www.nytimes.com/interactive/2019/12/19/opinion/location-tracking-cell-phone.html

71

https://www.forbes.com/sites/stevemccaskill/2019/06/12/la-liga-handed-e250000-gdpr-fine-for-spying-on-fans-watching-pirated-streams/

72 https://privacyinternational.org/report/2647/how-apps-android-share-data-facebook-report

73 https://www.telegraph.co.uk/news/2019/12/01/china-makes-face-scanning-compulsory-mobile-phone-owners/

74 https://gs.statcounter.com/os-market-share/mobile/worldwide

75 https://www.tomsguide.com/us/android-privacy-vs-iphone,news-27856.html

76 https://www.theverge.com/2021/3/8/22319136/whatsapp-cloud-backups-icloud-google-drive-password-encryption-security

77 https://arstechnica.com/tech-policy/2019/04/illinois-bill-banning-eavesdropping-by-iot-devices-defanged-by-tech-lobby/

78 https://mashable.com/article/ring-halloween-surveillance

79 https://www.cnet.com/home/smart-home/amazon-rings-police-partnerships-troubled-security-industry-group/

80 https://www.independent.co.uk/tech/amazon-ring-video-doorbell-police-warrant-b2122376.html

81 https://www.eff.org/deeplinks/2021/06/understanding-

amazon-sidewalk

[82]  https://www.techradar.com/news/google-fesses-up-to-nest-secures-undisclosed-microphone

[83]  https://www.voiceofwales.com/uk-government-to-store-all-smart-meter-data/

[84]  https://privacyinternational.org/news-analysis/2234/privacy-win-us-court-says-fourth-amendment-protects-smart-meter-data

[85]  https://www.independent.co.uk/tech/smart-tv-hack-fbi-cyber-stalk-camera-microphone-internet-a9230176.html

[86]  https://www.telegraph.co.uk/technology/2016/11/03/fitness-trackers-breaking-privacy-laws-says-watchdog/

[87]  https://www.thesun.ie/tech/4468545/even-your-xbox-is-spying-on-you-as-microsoft-admits-its-staff-listened-to-conversations-in-your-home/

[88]  https://edition.cnn.com/2019/08/20/cars/mercedes-trackers-intl-scli/index.html

[89]  https://www.fleetnews.co.uk/news/manufacturer-news/2019/02/11/uk-carmakers-expect-to-own-connected-car-data

[90]  https://www.tesla.com/ownersmanual/modely/en_us/GUID-EDAD116F-3C73-40FA-A861-68112FF7961F.html

[91]  https://www.vice.com/en/article/pgwean/internet-of-things-teddy-bear-leaked-2-million-parent-and-kids-message-recordings

[92]  https://www.nytimes.com/2017/02/17/technology/cayla-talking-doll-hackers.html

[93]  https://nakedsecurity.sophos.com/2019/11/28/kids-smartwatch-security-tracker-can-be-hacked-by-anyone/

[94]  https://metro.co.uk/2016/09/13/smart-dildo-was-spying-

on-my-vagina-woman-claims-6126467/
95

https://www.theguardian.com/technology/2017/aug/31/hack
ing-risk-recall-pacemakers-patient-death-fears-fda-
firmware-update
96  https://coconuts.co/singapore/news/singapore-ranked-11-
in-most-surveilled-cities-in-the-world-study-comparitech/
97      https://www.independent.co.uk/news/uk/crime/facial-
recognition-london-met-police-scotland-yard-privacy-
a9299986.html
98

https://www.computerweekly.com/news/252471875/Home-
Office-picks-supplier-for-300m-biometrics-project
99      https://www.gov.uk/government/publications/national-
surveillance-camera-strategy-for-england-and-wales
100        https://www.thisismoney.co.uk/money/cars/article-
7201165/Londons-Big-Brother-cameras-catch-4-000-
moving-traffic-offences-day.html
101        https://www.bloomberg.com/news/articles/2019-07-
19/google-settles-privacy-case-over-street-view-for-13-
million
102 https://www.wired.com/2007/06/w-wifi-record-2/
103

https://www.theguardian.com/technology/2016/jan/21/shops
-track-smartphone-uk-privacy-watchdog-warns
104                    https://arstechnica.com/information-
technology/2013/10/nsa-repeatedly-tries-to-unpeel-tor-
anonymity-and-spy-on-users-memos-show/
105     https://www.reuters.com/technology/russia-ratchets-up-
internet-crackdown-with-block-privacy-service-tor-2021-
12-08/
106        https://www.csoonline.com/article/3305795/forcing-

users-to-log-into-google-chrome-without-consent-raises-privacy-concerns.html

[107]            https://gs.statcounter.com/browser-market-share/desktop/worldwide

[108] https://tosdr.org/

[109]

https://www.washingtonpost.com/technology/2020/01/28/off-facebook-activity-page/

[110]    https://krebsonsecurity.com/2019/03/facebook-stored-hundreds-of-millions-of-user-passwords-in-plain-text-for-years/

[111]    https://www.ncsc.gov.uk/news/most-hacked-passwords-revealed-as-uk-cyber-survey-exposes-gaps-in-online-security

[112]    https://www.techrepublic.com/article/why-you-should-never-allow-your-web-browser-to-save-your-passwords/

[113]       https://www.bloomberg.com/news/articles/2018-06-15/deleting-your-online-dna-data-is-brutally-difficult

[114]       https://www.nytimes.com/2019/11/05/business/dna-database-search-warrant.html

[115]        https://www.dw.com/en/germanys-data-chief-tells-ministries-whatsapp-is-a-no-go/a-53474413

[116]

https://www.theguardian.com/technology/2020/dec/23/amazon-ring-camera-hack-lawsuit-threats

[117]

https://www.forbes.com/sites/ajdellinger/2019/04/30/how-the-biggest-tech-companies-spent-half-a-billion-dollars-lobbying-congress/

[118] https://www.bankofengland.co.uk/the-digital-pound

[119]       https://falkvinge.net/2018/05/18/analog-equivalent-rights-conclusion-privacy-eliminated-digital-environment/

[120] https://www.businessinsider.com/neuralink-elon-musk-microchips-brains-ai-2021-2

[121] https://www.bmh.manchester.ac.uk/connect/social-responsibility/impact/bionic-eye-implant/

[122] https://futurism.com/mind-controlled-robotic-arm-johnny-matheny

[123] https://interestingengineering.com/innovation/nanobots-will-be-flowing-through-your-body-by-2030

[124] https://www.sciencealert.com/wealthy-humans-could-live-forever-as-cyborgs-within-200-years-expert-predicts

[125] https://www.theweek.co.uk/97695/major-uk-firms-to-microchip-employees

[126]
https://www.theverge.com/2019/2/28/18244632/facebook-political-debate-system-digital-forum-reputation-patent-filing

[127] https://www.gov.uk/government/speeches/pm-speech-to-the-un-general-assembly-24-september-2019

[128] https://en.wikipedia.org/wiki/Black_Mirror

Printed in Great Britain
by Amazon